Poor Relief in [

Two A-Level personal studies

1. A study of the English Poor Law from the early
   seventeenth to the late nineteenth century, and
   particularly in Abbotskerswell
   Susannah Wheeleker

2. Industrial and rural poor relief, 1919-29 :
   a comparison of Dudley and Totnes
   Sarah Eyles

Series editor — _Hugh Bodey_

**The Devonshire Association
for the Advancement of Science, Literature and the Arts**

First published in 1991 by
The Devonshire Association
7 The Close
Exeter
Devon

Origination and design by Ex Libris Press
1 The Shambles
Bradford on Avon
Wiltshire

Typeset in 9 and 11 point Palatino by
Manuscript, Trowbridge

Printed by Devenish & Company, Bath

ISBN 0 85214 048 7

Acknowlegements

The cover illustration is from a pencil drawing of the Exeter soup kitchen, drawn by G. Townsend in January,1861. Thanks are expressed to the Devon and Exeter Institution for providing this illustration from their collections, and to Gillian Bodey who typed the manuscript studies.

Contents

Series note

Some examining boards have been including a personal study as part of the examinations set at Advanced Level for some years. Though at first this was limited to a few subjects and fewer boards, the value of such studies educationally, personally and as a means of asssessment has caused the practice to spread.

Many of the studies students develop contain new information and it is the purpose of this series to make some of those relevant to Devon available to a wider public. The precise requirements of the boards vary, and an explanatory note precedes each study to allow the reader to realise the parameters within which the students have had to work. It would be unfair to the writers to compare one study with another as the requirements of the boards vary quite widely. The principal limitations common to all boards are a prescribed maximum length and the necessity to originate and develop the question to be researched, trace relevant sources, evaluate them and write a balanced synthesis all well within the two years of the course and with no possibility of an extension. Most students are 16 or 17 when they start an A-level course, and are studying other subjects as well. The finished studies frequently exceed expectation, and are a credit to the students concerned.

The studies also reflect well on the teachers who guide and advise the students. This kind of teaching is much more demanding than the traditional 'chalk and talk', since most boards allow candidates almost unlimited freedom in the choice of topic they wish to pursue. Any one group may well contain students studying minute aspects of any part of British history in the past two thousand years, or of the history of some other country, for it need not be British. At the same time studies of a biographical nature or even historiography may also appear. Teachers need to be well read, knowledgeable on research techniques and the availability of source material, ready to adapt from discussing the evidence for Roman house styles in south Devon with one student to the 'shaking Quakers' of America with the next and full of encouragement when the leads that the third was

4

pursuing run cold. The quality of the studies owe much to the skill and enthusiasm of the teachers, who see considerable educational benefits in such work.

The largest subject area producing studies at present is history, which determines the content of this booklet. However it is not intended that this series shall be limited to history; as many studies will be published as are of sufficient quality, of general interest to the people of Devon and as funds permit. Teachers and students are warmly invited to write to the series editor for a leaflet giving further details.

The inclusion of a study in a booklet does not imply that the Devonshire Association agrees with the views expressed nor that the student who wrote it was awarded any particular grade.

Hugh Bodey, Editor

A study of the poor laws in operation in England from the early seventeenth century to the late nineteenth century and how they operated on a local basis in the south Devon parish of Abbotskerswell —

Susannah Wheeleker

[Susannah wrote this study while she was preparing to take A-Level at Blundell's School, Tiverton. The study was written as part of the History syllabus offered by the Oxford and Cambridge Board. The course based on that syllabus is designed to stimulate interest in and promote the study of history: through the understanding and knowlege of selected periods or themes; through the consideration of the nature of historical sources and the methods used by historians and by promoting an awareness of change through time. The examination includes papers answered by essays and a study that is allocated 20% of the total mark. The study requires the candidate to use both primary and secondary sources to research a topic of her choice in depth, and to write a balanced synthesis. The completed study has to be about 5000 words and is followed by an oral examination in which the candidate is asked to reflect on the process and nature of historical research — *Editor*]

The national legislation

The Elizabethan Poor Law of 1601 established the basis of poor relief for over two centuries (until 1834) with only minor variations during this period. Prior to the Elizabethan statute the responsibility for the poor lay with the Church and the monasteries before their dissolution by Henry VIII, Elizabeth's father. It was only after 1601, when the Act combined the "best" of a century's previous legislation including the Act of 1536 under Cromwell, that the relief of the poor became a parish delegation.

Private charity could not be depended upon for the maintenance of the poor, therefore under the Act poor rates were to be levied on those who could afford them. The statute provided that the rates were to be spent in four main ways : 'for setting to work the children of all such whose parents shall not be thought able to maintain them', 'for setting to work all persons, married or unmarried, having no means to maintain them, and who use no ordinary or daily trade of life to get their living by', 'for providing a convenient stock of flax, hemp, wood, thread, iron and other ware and stuff to set the poor on work' and 'for the necessary relief of the lame, impotent, old, blind and such other among them being poor and not able to work.'[1]

The poor rate was ordered to be collected by the overseer of each parish — an unpaid and unpopular position appointed by the local Justice of the Peace. The collection of tax in the seventeenth and eighteenth centuries was no more popular than it is today.

In 1662 the Laws of Settlement confirmed the local character of poor relief. Any stranger to a parish who had no prospect of work within forty days or did not rent a property to the value of £10 per annum could be removed from the parish by the overseer. Any person wishing to settle in a new parish had to submit a claim for settlement to be heard by local magistrates. Any person employed in casual labour, for example during the harvest period, had to obtain a certificate from his home parish guaranteeing to take him back when his work was complete.

The victory of Parliament, sealed in 1689, brought a new concept of public administration just as the Reformation and the subsequent rise of puritanism had brought a harsher element into social thinking. Charity was dampened by the new concepts of diligence and thrift. Poverty was looked upon as idleness and irresponsibilty.

Although no major alterations had been made to the original Act of 1601, parliament continued to pass minor pieces of legislation amending what had gone before with the object of alleviating problems of administering poor relief. Two such acts were passed in the latter part of the seventeenth century. The first in 1691 enacted that a register of parishioners in receipt of poor relief should be kept. The second, the Settlement Act of 1697, permitted strangers to settle in a new parish if they were in possession of a certificate from their home parish stating that it would take them back should they become in need of poor relief. Under that Act, paupers had to wear the pauper badge — a capital 'P', followed by a letter to indicate the name of their parish.

When in their own parish, persons wishing to apply for relief had to apply to the overseer of the poor or to the local magistrate. In 1722 an act was passed to make the administration of poor relief more strict. It stated that all applications for relief should be made to the overseer first and if this was refused the claimant could apply to the magistrate who could overrule the overseer and grant relief. Under the Act parishes could 'farm out' the poor to an employer.

Poor relief throughout the centuries came in two forms, outdoor and indoor relief. Outdoor relief was paid as a weekly pension or 'dole' whereas indoor relief came in the much detested shape of the workhouse.

Before 1723 a special Act of Parliament had to be obtained by any parish wishing to build a workhouse. The Knatchbull General Workhouse Act of 1723 empowered overseers, with the consent of the vestry, to erect workhouses in single parishes. The Act also permitted several smaller parishes to join together in a Union to make such a building viable. The declared purpose of these workhouses was to put the poor to work and the measure led to a stringent workhouse test: any claimant of poor relief who refused to enter the workhouse forfeited his right to any relief whatsoever. By 1776 there were reported to be over two thousand workhouses in England, proving their popularity as an economical way of dealing with the poor.

The latter half of the eighteenth century saw a radical alteration in social attitudes. Artists, writers and public figures alike began to notice the plight of the less fortunate, leading to a political response. Gilbert's Act of 1782 eased some of the harshness of the workhouse test and encouraged parishes to combine with others to form unions. Inspectors were appointed on a local basis to check on conditions in the workhouses. Able-bodied paupers were to be found work outside the workhouse and orphaned children were boarded out. Paupers of good character were no longer obliged to wear the pauper badge. However this Act was voluntary and by 1834 only 924 parishes out of 16,000 had taken advantage of it.

In 1795, Pitt ensured that the Laws of Settlement were relaxed and it was in the same year that the Berkshire Justices assembled at the Pelican Inn in Speenhamland near Newbury and decided to regulate poor relief in accordance with the price of bread and the size of a man's family. It was 'resolved unanimously that the present state of the poor does require further assistance than has generally been given them'. The supplement to workers' wages was fixed as follows:

'When the Gallon Loaf of Second Flour, weighing 8lb 11oz, shall cost 1 shilling, then every poor and industrious man shall have for his own support 3s. weekly either produced by his own or his family's labour, or an allowance from the poor rates, and for the support of his wife and every other of his family, 1s. 6d.

When the Gallon Loaf shall cost 1s. 4d. then every poor and industrious man shall have 4s. weekly for his own, and 1s. 10d for the support of every other of his family.

And so in proportion, as the price of bread rises or falls (that is to say) 3d. to the man and 1d. to every other of his family, on every 1d. which the loaf rises above 1s.' [2]

The Speenhamland system was widely adopted, once parliamentary authority had been obtained. The appalling effects of enclosure on the agricultural labouring population had been realized by many

9

landowners and the spread of the system into industrial areas proved the general concern for good order, even though it was a more expensive system than had been used before. Indeed, in one parish alone in southern England, the poor rate increased from £18 per annum to £367 in just thirty years. It may, however, have been a price the ratepayers were willing to pay to avoid revolution and uprisings.

The Poor Law was not just concerned with the provision of relief for the poor, it also ensured the provision of employment for paupers. Schemes for putting the poor to work included the labour rate, common in small parishes where the ratepayers bound themselves to provide employment at a given rate to those who were unable to find it, and the roundsman system, prevalent in Oxfordshire, Berkshire and Buckinghamshire, under which the labourers went round a parish with a ticket ordering the farmers to employ them. Under this system the parish subsidised the wages from the parish fund. In Oxfordshire, the labourers of some parishes were auctioned once a year. The farmer whose bid came closest to the price fixed by the parish secured the services of the man he bid for.

The increasing pressure of poverty became more evident as more pieces of legislation were brought into being to deal with the problem. In 1796 an Act, of which Sir William Young was the author, was passed which replaced the 1722 Act and abolished the restriction of the right to relief of persons willing to enter the workhouse and provided that claimants for poor relief could apply directly to a magistrate. The Act declared that the restrictions had been found inconvenient and oppressive. Pitt, at the turn of the eighteenth century, wanted to reform the whole system of poor relief but he failed because his scheme was confused, incoherent, and in places impracticable. Advocates of *laissez faire*, such as Richards, underlined the necessity of a low-wage economy, which Speenhamland clearly controverted. Malthus believed the only way to relieve poverty was to increase it and thus create a separate pauper population. Ratepayers, industrialists and landowners alike were all caught up in the demands for a new method of relief and increased harshness in its administration.

There was a severe agricultural depression in 1830. The resulting high unemployment was made worse when justices of the peace tried to reduce the poor rate burden for farmers, whose corn was selling at much lower prices than in previous years. This was to be achieved by reducing the scale and quantum of relief. The result of this was widespread rioting in 1830 and 1831. The Government's view was that the system which had led men to expect poor relief as the norm was 'demoralising the populace'. Accordingly a Poor Law Commission was appointed to look into the question of poverty and the effects of the Poor Law.

The commission ignored the causes of distress and the problems of the industrial towns, all the blame was laid upon the Speenhamland system. The commission was unimpressed by the efficient and economical running of the workhouse system. The recommendations were that able-bodied persons should no longer be entitled to outdoor relief and that the workhouse should become the central element of the new system. In an effort to deter people from seeking relief, workhouses were to be as discouraging and more unattractive than 'the situation of the independent labourer of the lowest class'. There were to be separate workhouses for children, men, women and the infirm. Therefore married couples and families were split up, no communication was allowed between members of the same family and only infrequent reunions were permitted. The Poor Law Commission was to administer the Poor Law, and assistant commissioners were appointed for local inspections. Boards of Guardians were responsible for the running of the system at a local level.

The Poor Law Amendment Act was passed in 1834 and embodied the recommendations of the commission. The three commissioners were T. Frankland Lewis, J. G. Shaw Lefevre and George Nichols. They soon became known as 'the Three Kings of Somerset House', the location of their offices. Once the legislation began to take effect they were as hated as the 'Bastilles', the name given to the workhouses by the people.

The threat of the workhouse encouraged the able-bodied to find work, and prevented 'scrounging' from the parish which low paid workers had resented under the old system. It was understandable that they should feel like this because before they had been working for almost the same wage as the paupers had received from the parish for doing nothing. Apart from encouraging work, the new law provided a limited education for pauper children as well as teaching them a trade.

The Poor Law led to a substantial drop in poor relief expenditure, as the table below shows. This was due to the decrease in the amount of outdoor relief being paid out and the increase in the number of workhouses being used to deal with the poor.

Year ending Lady Day	Expended Poor Relief	Rate per head
1831	£6,798,889	9s 9d
1835	£5,526,418	7s 7d
1836	£4,717,630	6s 4³/₄d
1841	£4,760,929	6s 0¹/₂d
1850	£5,395,022	6s 1d
1851	£4,962,704	5s 6¹/₂d

However, there were problems with the new system. It was not operable in areas of high unemployment and there were widespread riots in towns where workhouses were to be built.

In 1847 the Poor Law Commission was replaced by the Poor Law Board and the Poor Law regulations were relaxed and outdoor relief could once again be provided for the able bodied. These changes were the first major steps to be taken in reorganising the system of pauper relief in England since 1601.

There is no doubt that the changes made to the original Poor Law had a great effect on the country as a whole but different towns and parishes operated in different ways with local variations and interpretations of each law and act. Even neighbouring parishes differed in the way they handled their own paupers. It is therefore important to consider the effect that the Poor Law had on a local scale.

The Operation of the Poor Laws in the South Devon Parish of Abbotskerwell

Abbotskerswell is a village situated two miles to the south of Newton Abbot in south Devon. It is no longer an independent parish but was throughout the eighteenth and nineteenth centuries. There exist for this parish a number of documents relating to the local operation of the poor laws. Such documents include the overseers account books, the register of parish apprentices, settlement indentures and bastardy documents dating from the early eighteenth century to the mid-nineteenth century. These documents give a clearer picture of how the local poor rate was spent, which families were the most needy and how the national changes affected a small village community.

The placing of apprentices was arranged by the overseer of the poor. The children of the poor of Abbotskerswell were placed, for a fee of ten shillings (50p), with a master in a neighbouring parish. It was not uncommon for children as young as six to be bound to their master until they were twenty-one, although girls could end their terms sooner should they wish to get married. The churchwarden and overseers had to approve of the master before any children could be placed with him but there was no way of monitoring the subsequent progress of the children. Some reports from parishes near Abbotskerswell reveal acts of great cruelty towards apprentices. as for example the case of Mary Puddicombe who was apprenticed as a servant for two years at Blackiston after her first master died. She told the Poor Law Commissioners for the purpose of a report into the employment of women and children in agriculture:

> I was treated very bad there, the people beat their servants. I used to be beat black and blue... One maiden had her arm cut to the bone with a stick the young master cut out of the hedge at the time...

Such was the treatment of apprentices in many parishes all over Devon. However, on March 24, 1834, all entries in the register of

13

parish apprentices stopped and there are no further records of any apprenticeships after this date. This is presumably because of the Poor Law Amendment Act and the subsequent opening of the workhouse in Newton Abbot in 1839.

Another matter dealt with by the parish was that of illegitimate babies of poor mothers. The father had to be discovered and was then obliged to enter into a bond to pay a shilling or more a week towards the upkeep of the child, failing which he could be arrested. Enquiry was by complaint before the local magistrate.

The account books of the parish overseers reveal much about the poor of Abbotskerswell, how the poor rates were levied and how the money was distributed in the parish. It is possible to go back as far as 1700 to examine the payments to and the treatment of the poor in the parish.

In 1700 the rate to be levied for the relief of the poor was £6. 13s. 7d. The rate was based on properties. For example, Thomas Lyn Good paid the highest sum of 7s 10d, the vicar paid 4s and the lowest contribution was 2d. In 1700, £8. 8s. 7d was carried over as a balance from previous years. This balance, added to the rate, collected only once in 1700, provided £15. 2s. 2d for the relief of the poor. Of this sum, £13. 14s. was paid to the poor altogether. There were 36 recorded 'disbersments' to two families in receipt of relief.

Fifty years later, in 1750, the rate payable by the parishioners was still levied at £6. 13s. 7d but instead of being an annual payment it was now quarterly. The rate paid by individuals was no greater than in 1700: the vicar was still paying 4s per rate but demand for relief was such that the rate had to be collected four times that year.

There were 66 disbursements in 1750 which amounted to £27. 10s. 6d (compared with the 36 disbursements totalling £13. 14s. fifty years earlier). These were funded as follows:

	£	s	d
Four Rates	26	14	4
Recd. at the last Overseers	2	2	$5^1/2$
Recd. for some poors cloaths		2	6
	£28	19	$3^1/2$

So there Remains Due to the Next Overseers £1. 8s. $9^1/_2$d

The recipients of the rate were not all paupers. Wages for work undertaken for the poor, or the parish, were also paid from the poor rate. For example,in 1750 the following payment was made:

Elizabeth Strong, for washing the poors
cloaths 24 weeks — 8s

Not only were the poor costly to the parish during their lives but when they died the funeral costs also had to be met by the parish. Also in 1750:

Laying fourth of Mary Jolard	4s
For a shroud and making	2s
For the coffing	8s
For making the grave	2s
	16s

From the account books it becomes clear that certain families were a regular burden to the parish. In an extract from the 1750 entries it is clear that the Newton family were in receipt of most of the 66 disbursements for that year, including:

A pair of shoes for Will Newton	3s 6d
Taping of Newton's shoes leather and nails	1s 0d
For cutting of Newton's shoes	3d
Pr. of stockings for Newton	1s 6d
A hat for Newton	1s 5d
3 yards and $^3/_4$ of cloth for a shirt for Newton and making	3s 0d
Pair briches for Will Newton	2s 6d

And so the entries continue, including more payments for the mending and provision of clothes, shoes and stockings for the Newton family. Even the shaving of Will Newton and Samuel

Laverton is recorded, at a cost of 2s.

Nearly two decades later, in 1768, the Sheriff of Devon, George Fursdon of Cadbury, summoned a county meeting of gentlemen, clergy and freeholders in Exeter and laid before it a scheme for the establishment of a system of social insurance throughout the county. The scheme was to be voluntary and available to every inhabitant between the ages of 21 and 41 years. It was embodied in a private Act of Parliament passed in 1769. This first attempt at social insurance was remarkable for the comprehensiveness of its benefits. It was also weighted heavily in favour of the poorer classes, who were to receive greater benefits in proportion to their subscriptions than the more well to do.

The scheme suffered from the defect that it was voluntary and not all parishes adopted it. Even in those parishes that did adopt the scheme the wealthier inhabitants did not join in sufficient numbers to keep the funds solvent. Consequently, after three years it became necessary to call another meeting where it was unanimously decided to petition for the repeal of the Act. There is, however, no record of the adoption of this Act by the members of the parish of Abbotskerswell. It was, however a brave attempt by the officials of Devon to do something to alleviate the problems of the poor in their own county.

Parish matters were undertaken in a limited democratic way in Abbotskerswell, the limitation being that to vote on parish matters one had to be a ratepayer. Whenever there was a decision to be made that concerned the parish a meeting of ratepayers was called. For example, on October 21, 1773, at a meeting of parishoners it was unanimously agreed that,

all Felonies, Burglaries and Capital Crimes committed within the Parish of Abbotskerswell be prosecuted at the expense of the Parish and the charges for any such Prosecutions be paid out of the Poor rate.

With the added cost of prosecution proceedings, warrants and other such expenses in addition to actual relief payments it became necessary to collect more money for poor relief.

By 1793 whilst the rate to be collected from parishoners remained at £6 13s 7d it was collected eleven times that year (as compared to once 93 years earlier and four times 43 years earlier), giving an income of £86 6s $0^1/_2$ for relief. By 1820 £263 2s·$3^1/_2$ was required for disbursements in the village so the rate was collected 42 times in that year. From this time onwards the amount collected for poor relief remained relatively constant, although the account books reveal an 'overspend' in 1825 which had to be rectified the following year.

Apart from the actual account books documents such as those relating to the 'Legal parish of abode of applicants for relief', the so called settlement examinations, provide an interesting insight into the lives of people who needed poor relief. Where there was any doubt as to a person's past the individual had to swear details of any past employment and places of residence. In some cases they show a surprising mobility. For example, an examination of William Manley of July 1, 1779, shows he was born near Taunton in Somerset and was apprenticed to a wheelwright in Wellington before moving to Walborough and Ipplepen in south Devon, practicing his trade there for 11 shillings a week before marrying and settling in Abbotskerswell. James Watkins in 1801 stated on enquiry that he was born in Abergavenny in Monmouthshire before going on as a journeyman cordwainer (shoemaker) to Monmouth, with two breaks while he served as a substitute in the North Gloucester Militia, after which he came to Abbotskerswell where he married.

Perhaps the most suprising examination was of Thomas Leaker. In 1810 he said that he had been born in the parish and, when about 15 years old, bound himself apprentice to William Henley of Highweek, south Devon, for five years 'in the sea service'. The area around Newton Abbot was used to recruit seaman for the Newfoundland cod fishing industry. Leaker went fishing there each summer, returning with his master to Highweek each winter. But after four years he was 'taken by the French at sea and carried into a prison in

France'. Later he was exchanged but was then pressed into the Navy where he served a further six years before returning to the merchant service. Finally he returned to Abbotskerswell but having fallen on hard times, and despite service and imprisonment for his country, still had to prove his right of abode to claim relief.

As the numbers of paupers in need of relief increased the need for a different system of dealing with the poor became evident. In 1836 a meeting was held at the Globe Inn in Newton Abbot, as reported in the *Exeter Flying Post* of June 23, 1836. It was at that meeting that the decision was taken to replace the old Newton workhouse with a new Union. This new Union was comprised of 39 Parishes, including Abbotskerswell, covering 184 square miles and 44,358 people living in 8,528 houses. Three years prior to the opening of the Union the poor relief expenditure for that area was £16,756, this dropped to £12,928 after the workhouse opened.

The workhhouse itself housed 400 inmates and was the largest west of Bristol. The building and furnishing of it cost £13,000. It provided two acres of woodland and yards and a further two acres of garden. It was, theoretically, a model example of how the poor should be kept together and work under one roof. However, things were not as they appeared.

In 1872 Dr.J.W.Ley exposed the abuses of the workhouse system locally and forced a public inquiry which showed that the inmates 'suffered from lack of attention, the food was unsuitable and there was no proper separation of children and the mentally ill'. The *Western Times* reported:

Dr Ley, who is still a member of the Board, and in spite of blindness has attended meetings to the end, informed our representative that his greatest difficulty was to obtain corroborative evidence of what was going on. It was one of his allegations that there was not a single trained nurse in any of the institutions in the county, and he made a great stir by alleging that inmates were being tied down in their beds unable to move in jumpers or sacks made of sail cloth.

The report, following the inquiry, found 'that both the majority of the Guardians and all their officers have altogether failed to appreciate the serious responsibilities that rest upon them as regards the welfare of the inmates under their care'.

As a result of this scandal all the services of the then resident staff were dispensed with. £37,515 was borrowed for the improvement of the workhouse, including the building of a new infirmary of 172 beds which today forms part of Newton Abbot hospital.

This was the operation of the Poor Laws on a local scale. In Abbotskerswell there were no major problems in the management of the poor. The national legislation did not really affect the parish in any significant way, the basic system of collecting and distributing a poor rate was adequate until the opening of the Newton Abbot Union which undoubtedly relieved some of the pressures from the parish.

Throughout the centuries there have been various schemes to help alleviate the problems of the poor. Much depended upon the social attitudes of the time as to how the poor were to be treated. Although many systems were introduced on a national scale they were not always adopted by every parish in the country which meant that there was no organised nationwide system for the relief of the poor. The workhouse system was the closest to a national solution but, as proved in Newton Abbot, was the least humane system.

The schemes that were introduced were not ideal but were the best that could be established at the time. Out of all the systems that were put into practice the most suitable turned out to be the one that was introduced in the very first pieces of legislation to do with the poor. This was the system whereby poor rates were collected and used to help the poor. The proof of this system's success is the fact that we use a similar system today, only in a more sophisticated form, that of social security benefits.

The treatment of the poor throughout the centuries can be summed up in the words of Oliver Goldsmith in his play *The Traveller*:

"Laws grind the poor and rich men rule the Law."

References

1 J. Richardson, *The Local Historian's Encyclopaedia*
2 R. C. Birch, *The Shaping of the Welfare State*
3 J. Richardson, *The Local Historian's Encyclopaedia*

Bibliography

Primary Sources:
Abbotskerswell Overseers Account Books 1694-1793; 1819-1837
Abbotskerswell Register of Parish Apprentices 1803-1837
Abbotskerswell Bastardy Examinations 1735-1835
Abbotskerswell Settlement Examinations 1796-1823
Abbotskerswell Indentuies of Apprentices 1807-1825
Various articles from *The Exeter Flying Post*
Various articles from *The Western Times*

Secondary Sources:
The shaping of the Welfare State: R.C.Birch
Early Victorian England Volumes 1 and 2: Young
England 1807-1914: Ensor
English Country Life 1780-1830: E.W.Bovill
The Village Labourer 1760-1832: J.L.and B Hammond
Devonshire Studies: W.G Hoskins and H.Finberg
Newton Abbot: Derek Beavis
Newton Abbot: Roger Jones
Newton Abbot: Rhodes
Devon and Cornwall Queries
Devon Historian: April 1975 and 1976 editions
Various *Kelly's Directories*
Report and Transactions of the Devonshire Association, vol XCVI

The Devonshire Association was formed in 1862 to encourage the study of science, literature and the arts within the county. The Association began publishing the results of such study from the start, producing its first 'Transactions' in 1862. 'Transactions' have continued in an unbroken series ever since and regularly contain a wide variety of papers that are themselves the basis of research around the world. The Association also publishes other work which throws new light on the county, as much about its present as its past.

Further information about these publications, about the lectures, visits and study weeks arranged by the Association and about personal or corporate membership are available from —
The Registrar, The Devonshire Association, 7 The Close, Exeter EX1 1EZ, England.

Industrial and rural poor relief, 1919-29: a comparative study of Totnes and Dudley — *Sarah Eyles*

[This comparative study was prepared when Sarah was a student at South Devon College of Arts and Technology, as part of the Associated Examining Board's history syllabus 673. The course based on History Syllabus 673 is designed to stimulate interest in and promote the study of history: through the understanding and knowledge of selected periods or themes; through the consideration of the nature of historical sources and the methods used by historians and by promoting an awareness of change through time. The examination is made up of three components: a study of a selected period of time examined by essays; an investigation of historical method and of the nature of history, examined by both essays and source analysis; and the personal study. The study requires the candidate to use both primary and secondary sources to research a topic of her choice in depth, and to write a balanced synthesis. The completed study has to be between 4000 and 6000 words, and has to include a statement of aims, a bibliography and, ideally, footnotes to the sources used. Candidates are asked to consider, with the benefit of hindsight, how the study might have been handled differently. The study accounts for 25% of the total mark — Editor]

Aims

In my personal study I intend to take a look at poor relief, concentrating on the period 1919-29. To help me with this, I have chosen to look at two different areas — Totnes, a rural town in Devon, and Dudley, an industrial town in the West Midlands. By looking at statistics for the two different areas I hope to make a comparison, for example was poor relief as extensive in Totnes as in Dudley and were the numbers in the workhouses affected by the seasons or by trade? I also hope to compare the two towns to the national scene.

Life in the workhouse
(Written from Newmarket Union in 1846)

Since I cannot dear sister with you hold communion
I'll give you a sketch of our life in the Union.
But how to begin I don't know, I declare .
Let me see: well the first is our grand bill of fare .
We've skully for breakfast, at night bread and cheese
And we eat it and then go to bed if you please.
Two days in the week we have puddings for dinner
And two we have broth so like water but thinner
Two, meat and potatoes, of this none to spare
One day, bread and cheese and this is our fare.

And now then my clothes I will try to portray.
They are made of coarse cloth and the colour is grey.
My jacket and waistcoat don't fit me at all.
My shirt is too short or I am too tall.
My shoes are not pairs though of course I have two,
They are down at the heel and my stockings are blue.
A sort of skotch bonnet we wear on our heads,
And I sleep in a room where there are just fourteen beds,
Some are sleeping, some snoring, some talking, some playing,
Some fighting, some swearing, but very few praying.

There are nine at a time who work on the mill
We take it in turns so it never stands still,
A half hour each gang, so tis not very hard,
And when we are off we can walk in the yard.
I sometimes look up to the bit of blue sky,
High over my head, with a tear in my eye
Surrounded by walls that are too high to climb,
Confined like a felon without any crime,
Not a field, nor a house, nor a hedge can I see,
Not a plant, not a flower, nor a bush, nor a tree,
But I'm getting I find too pathetic by half,
And my object was only to cause you to laugh.
So my love to yourself, your husband and daughter,
I'll drink to your health in a tin of cold water.
Of course we've no wine, nor porter, nor beer
So you see that we are all teetotallers here.[1]

The new Poor Law — a brief history

Before 1834, poor relief in Britain was very disorganised and very expensive. Almost anyone could receive relief and it was often difficult to tell if people were genuine or not. Most began to believe that wage supplements were a right and this resulted in poor relief rising to as much as £7,900,000 in 1818. It was obvious that a solution had to be found to reduce such a huge burden on the rates and to spend money more wisely.

In 1834 the Poor Law Amendment Act was passed. One principle of the act was that outdoor relief for the able-bodied would cease, for example the Speenhamland system. Instead anyone who was fit enough to work went into a workhouse. The conditions inside workhouses were to be made less eligible than the lowest paid working conditions outside. Families would be worse off than the poorest poor as far as food and conditions were concerned. In these workhouses families were to be split up. The sick, infirm and those over 60 years old were the only ones able to receive outdoor relief.

Parishes were to be grouped together into Poor Law Unions with boards of guardians and they were to employ paid officials. A Board of Commissioners was set up in London to supervise local officials and to inspect poor relief to see the law was being carried out correctly. The parish had to provide detailed reports and the unions had to build workhouses. The standards of poor relief had to rise and people had to be encouraged to stand on their own two feet. Anybody who was workshy and idle had to change!

The Act was successful in that it did what it was intended to do: it cut the cost of poor relief by almost half even though the population was still growing during this period. Within five years the system had extended to 95% of parishes covering 85% of the population. After 1834 an estimated 350 new union workhouses were built or altered in order to accommodate the new classification of inmates. As the English countryside became accustomed to the sight of the workhouse, tales of related cruelty and horror spread throughout the land.

The *Times* newspaper reported endless stories of cruelty inside the workhouse. For example at Crediton two paupers, Locke and Dart, were confined to an unheated, damp, windowless, flowerless, bedless, outhouse and were one winter's day taken to the courtyard to be mopped with cold water. The *Times* also reported cases of inadequate outdoor relief.[2]

Many people were more prepared to starve to death or commit suicide than enter the workhouse. Historians such as Halevy saw commissioners as deliberately making it impossible for paupers to obtain relief, while Beatrice and Sydney Webb said the workhouses were shocking to every principle of reason and every feeling of humanity.

However while such comments may hold elements of truth, the annual reports of the Poor Law Commissioners after 1835 present an entirely different view. The new Poor Law Institution, according to them, brought about improvements, such as less pauperism, higher wages for groups such as farm labourers, more industrious workers, better treatment of the aged, finer schooling and better medical aid.

The workhouses were not 'bastilles'. Their diets were nutritious and their quarters as comfortable as the average labourer. Medical relief was generous and efficient and corporal punishment, except for the pauper boys, was outlawed. The separation of husbands and wives was found to be necessary in all public institutions over Europe. So superior indeed was the workhouse to the cottages of the poor that the only way to make them less eligible was by the enforcement of such rules as silence at meals.

The Poor Law in the Twentieth Century
As the years progressed out of the nineteenth century and into the twentieth, certain benefits were introduced at various stages designed to help in the relief of certain groups in society facing hardship.

In 1908 old age pensions came into existence, and their extension in 1925 guaranteed a basic income of ten shillings per week and one pound for a married couple living together. These pensions helped prevent to a certain degree the utter destitution that before 1914 had resulted in up to half of the elderly in some areas being forced to end their days in the workhouses — however the pension on its own fell below the existing poverty line — graphs 4a, 4b

Many widows who were claiming a widow's pension actually found themselves not only without their husband but also in a state of poverty. This is evident in the Dudley Union: see graph 4a, which compares men and women receiving out-relief. Normally if women earned more than a small amount they forfeited their widow's pension, and were condemned to finding low paid menial work.

The National Insurance Act came into operation fully by the end of 1913. It originally covered approximately twelve million workers but by 1925 it had extended to cover fifteen million.

The scheme provided a free general practitioner service and sickness benefit paid through 'approved societies' such as trade unions and benefit clubs. Local insurance committees could also distribute benefit to the dependants of insured workers requiring sanatorium treatment, though in general only insured workers could obtain free advice and treatment. Consequently worker's families had to be protected through private schemes and sick clubs.

Mass unemployment merely added to the number of families living in poverty and although generally alleviated by some form of unemployment insurance or parish relief, it could depending on the circumstances of families and individuals, still mean chronic hardship. Families usually lived on a weekly cycle from pay day to pay day.

By the winter of 1921-22 more than two million people were out of work in the United Kingdom. There was only a slow recovery throughout the 1920's.

The problem of unemployment was felt badly by those injured in the first world war. If disabled they were allowed a pension but the amount depended upon which part rendered them disabled, for example:-

The loss of a whole right arm	16s
Arm lost below shoulder but above elbow	14s
If below elbow pension was	11s 6d

(The loss of left arms was worth one shilling less than right arms.)

Thus a formerly skilled man would be forced to seek employment to supplement his pension if 'crippled' by the loss of his fingers or hand. Indeed many were forced into marginal employment such as selling matches, bootlaces or newspapers or in some cases simply begging.

Seasonal variations also affected unemployment in industrial towns in the 1920's. Unemployment tended to rise 10-15% in the winter compared to summer months.

In 1921, the majority of workers and their dependants were covered by the National Insurance Scheme. When Britain first began to experience mass unemployment in 1921-2, unemployment benefit offered about one third of the average wage, with six weeks of contribution required for each week of benefit, up to a maximum of fifteen weeks. Workers had to prove themselves available for work by 'signing on' every day at the labour exchange during working hours.

For the summer of 1921, an unemployed man over eighteen could receive fifteen shillings for himself, plus five shillings for a wife and one shilling for each child. However several large groups of workers lay outside the provision of National Insurance. These were mainly agricultural workers, domestic servants and the self-employed and without any other means of support these groups had to rely upon the poor law, usually in the form of 'out relief' or by entering the workhouse. By looking at graph 5, we can see that in the Dudley area there was always more unskilled than skilled workers entering the workhouse. But the insurance scheme soon ran into difficulties as the number of unemployed rose and the periods of unemployment became so great that increasingly large numbers of workers were thrown onto the poor law.

In 1927, applicants for unemployment benefit had to show that they were 'genuinely seeking work'. This phrase had originally been introduced in 1921 as an additional test of eligibility for the benefits to be paid after the standard forms of insurance had run out. However in 1927 it applied to all unemployment benefit, thus placing the unemployed in a vulnerable position: proof of entitlement now lay with them alone. To the unemployed man or woman these regulations were often a humiliating farce and an increasing occurrence as unemployment in some areas continued to grow — it is believed that many claimants were deprived of benefit in the late 1920's due to unsympathetic officials refusing on flimsy pretexts. However, although unemployment insurance kept most cases of the unemployed off the poor law, thus saving them from the stigma and humiliation that it carried, it was believed that by the end of the 1920's two suicides a day were the result of the depression and apathy that unemployment and poverty created in men.

By the 1920's many of the harshnesses of the nineteenth century poor law had been mitigated by the more generous provision of 'out door relief'. Even so, anywhere between one third and a fifth of those dying in the larger cities and towns could expect to end their days in the workhouse. Many feared old age, infirmity and destitution due to the still humiliating conditions provided for those relieved. Graph 3a shows how a large proportion of those in the workhouse were over 70 years. Regardless of the many schemes introduced during these periods the poor law, whether in the form of 'outdoor relief' or the workhouse, still remained an essential last resort in the case of those who had no other resources on which to call.

Up to date recollections from those remembering the 1920's often view the years with fond nostalgia mainly because of the bond felt between people due to the struggle to make ends meet.

An interview with Gladys Homer, a woman from Dudley, paints a fairly optimistic picture. She remembers two years of hardship when her husband, who was a machine worker, became unemployed. Her husband received 22 shillings from " the labour" with an extra two shillings when their son was born.

Before she married, Gladys used to work at Lench's of Blackheath but they were not in favour of keeping married women on, in fact mothers used to take it for granted that they left once they had children.

Although extremely hard up when her husband was out of work, Gladys used to do a number of jobs in order to make ends meet. On Mondays, 8am - 6pm, she washed, starched, dried and ironed washing at a neighbouring house for two shillings. She also took washing in at her own home and washed and dried that for two shillings. These extra amounts of money helped to buy food such as a sheep's head, which would last for two days, a joint of beef costing two shillings, or cows udders, etc.

Rent was four shillings per week, but apparently if she could not afford to pay it that week the rent man did not mind.

Gladys also recalled that the pawn brokers were put to good use and that her brother's wife

used to take bundles to the pawn-brokers for other people who were too proud to go and for a few pennies she would fetch it back again for them on a Saturday when the money came in.

With reference to the workhouse and other related poor law bodies, Gladys believed that on the whole people and families "stuck together". If people were badly off, their neighbours would help by giving food. She believed that if someone ended up in the workhouse then they must have been either dreadfully destitute or without a caring family or friends.[4]

Even so in 1920 there were 270,569 inmates in various poor law institutions and by the mid-1920's, between 350,000 and 450,000 unemployed people received relief under poor law provisions. In the worst years, such as the aftermath of the General Strike, as many as one and half million people were making claims on the poor law.

Indoor relief was becoming a heavy burden on the poor rates and for the hardest hit localities the cost of providing for the unemployed was absorbing as much as half of all poor law expenditure by the late 1920's, putting extreme strains on the local rating system. In addition, since the Great War, there had been friction between the central government and local boards of guardians about the level of relief. In 1926, Neville Chamberlain, as Minister of Health, had taken powers to replace local guardians who paid out too much relief. This led him in 1929 to include a reform of the Poor Law in his local Government Act in 1930 — this swept away the Poor Law Unions and the Boards of Guardians.

Thus it can be said that the six hundred Unions designed to serve the needs of an agricultural, uneducated and unenfranchised population of 14^1/$_2$ million had managed to survive well into an industrial age, an age of trade unions, the vote for each sex, education and a population of 38 million people.

Comparison of relief in Totnes and Dudley

Totnes is situated above the River Dart in South Devon. During the period I am studying Totnes was an agricultural town with agricultural based industries. These included the C & T Harris Ltd Bacon Factory, which also milled corn, and Daws' creameries. However these were not on a grand scale until after 1945.

As a result of the Poor Law Amendment Act, the workhouse at

Totnes was built. Work began in 1838 and it was completed in 1839 at a cost of £6,000. The building had room for 380 paupers. The Totnes Union covered 143 square miles, uniting the parishes of Ashprington, Berry Pomeroy, Brixham, Buckfastleigh, Churston Ferrers, Cornworthy, Dartington, St. Perox, St. Saviour and Townstal, in the Dartmouth Borough: Dean Prior, Diptford, Dittisham, Halwell, Harberton, Holne, Kingswear, Paignton, Rattery, South Brent, Staverton, Stoke Gabriel, Totnes and Ugborough. Totnes Union workhouse received its first inmates in 1839 from Brixham workhouse. During the first three years of the workhouse opening, the average annual expenditure was £13,183.

Dudley, by contrast, is an ancient industrial town in the newly created county of the West Midlands. Local industries included coal mining and steel, however during the inter-war years there was a crisis in the heavy industries.

The Dudley Union workhouse opened in June 1859. The sum of £1,500 was paid for the land on which it was going to stand alone. It covered the areas of Dudley town, Dudley county, Sedgley, Cosley, Tipton and Rowly Regis.

By looking at statistical evidence for the areas of Totnes and Dudley I intend to compare my results with what has already been written about the poor law in secondary sources. I also want to compare two very different Unions, Totnes being small in size and rural and Dudley being relatively large and industrial. My expectations are that there will be marked differences relating to seasons and trade. I chose the time span to get an overall picture of the inter-war years and to emphasize any seasonal fluctuations.

Looking at graphs 1a and 1b, of institutional relief only, both areas have a similar pattern. However there are differences towards the end of the time covered in the graphs. In the Dudley area institutional relief reached a peak in 1928, whilst institutional relief actually dropped in 1928 in Totnes. It seems strange that in an industrial area in the centre of the country, institutional relief rose. As the whole poor relief system ended in 1929 one would have thought that institutional relief would have been winding down.

The fact that institutional relief dropped in Totnes could mean that poor law inspectors were implementing forms of relief other than in the workhouse much more readily. This is indicated by the graphs showing statistics for poor relief other than institutional—graphs 2a, 2b. In Totnes the figures rose substantially in 1928 and in Dudley figures dropped. Looking at graphs 1a and 1b the pattern of those entering the workhouse did not change a great deal; there is either a gradual increase or decrease, there are no dramatic swings. It is interesting to see that there are no major seasonal fluctuations thus indicating that the number of poor stayed constant winter and summer. In industrial areas in the 1920s unemployment supposedly rose by 10 - 15% in the winter months. However, according to graphs 1a and 2a, statistics for Dudley show that in the summer months there was a slight increase of those receiving 'outdoor relief' and the pattern of those actually entering the workhouse did not decline either. The same applied to Totnes: in the months of August and September, a period when there should be more employment in agriculture, there was a slight rise in the number of people in the workhouse. However we can not come to any sound conclusions by just using evidence in the graphs. Other sources must be looked at, for example the extent of agriculture in Totnes.

In comparison to graphs 1(a) and 1(b), graphs 2(a) and (b) — "other than institutional relief" show much greater fluctuations. Figures for Totnes seem very erratic. Both graphs show an increase for the month of February, 1925. It is interesting to see that figures for Totnes drop substantially on the 15th August 1925, whilst in Dudley figures actually reach a peak. Despite so many fluctuations, the graph seems to indicate that Totnes inspectors afforded a greater number to have outdoor relief thus winding down the unsavoury task of institutionalizing the poor. In Dudley the fact that the poor law system was coming to an end did not seem to make much difference.

One problem when comparing the two areas is that I do not have a graph to show the number of poor in each area compared to the size of population. This would have been useful to see if there were more poor in Totnes or Dudley, which might then have given me a better understanding of the trends of the graphs. The remaining graphs add a certain amount of information about the respective areas, reinforcing the trends already mentioned[graphs 3a,3b]

It does seem that Totnes Union was more lenient, though again this cannot be proved without further evidence. The fact that Totnes workhouse was never full during the inter-war years does not mean that there were fewer poor. Families may have supported each other during times of hardship to avoid the shame of the workhouse or Totnes may have had other more specialised institutions at this time. By 1929 the numbers of those in workhouses equalled those in other homes for paupers. Evidence to support the trends of the graphs for Dudley, however can be found in the Dudley *Herald* for April 10, 1926.

Mr Evitt, who belonged to the Tipton poor law investigation committee said he spoke on behalf of the working class and intended to get fair play for all of his kind.

Mr Evitt said five years ago he became unemployed and applied for relief to the Dudley Guardians. A relieving officer visited him at his home and asked him "umpteen" questions, prying into his private concerns and he was even asked to produce a marriage licence. He had to appear before the Board of Guardians and after stating his case was told that the Guardians could do nothing for him as they had no scheme for helping the unemployed and was advised to take himself and his family into the workhouse.

Mr Evitt also gave figures of outrelief granted in the Dudley area and Birmingham poor law area. In Birmingham, he said, there were rent, coal and gas allowances in certain cases and children clothed and shod. In Dudley, the guardians had a scale but he had yet to find anyone who had been awarded the maximum.[5]

This newspaper article does seem to suggest, along with the statistics in the graphs, that Dudley Union still had harsh principles even in the late 1920s.

Conclusion

After studying the graphs for my personal study, I now realise that perhaps my time span was too long. The subject of the poor law is so vast and most of the available primary source material is statistical. This makes it difficult to explain any variations fully. I realise now that perhaps it would have been better to look at one year in detail. However I feel that by looking at a longer time span I have given a general picture of poor relief during the inter-war years and that the study was still worthwhile. By looking at primary and secondary source material I could make some conclusions about Dudley and Totnes and support or disagree to a certain extent with any conclusions made in secondary sources. Because the poor law is surrounded by so much controversy and debate, especially the inter-war years, secondary sources and primary sources have to be treated with caution. Because the subject is so emotive it is often difficult to be unbiased. For example, Beatrice and Sydney Webb who said the workhouses were 'shocking to every principle of reason and every feeling of humanity' were active socialists so they were not likely to be in favour of the poor law. In comparison commissioners' reports are not going to be unbiased either, it is clear that they held an optimistic view of the workhouse.

References

1 *The Workhouse*: Norman Longmate, 1974
2 The Poor Law folder — Dudley Archives. Taken from The *Times*, 19 Jan 1838.
3 E. Halery: *History of the English people in the 19th Century*
4 Interview, 1987, Dudley — Mrs Gladys Homer.
5 *Dudley Herald*, April 10th 1926 — Dudley Archives.

Bibliography

Primary Sources — from Dudley Archives:
Weekly returns of the Poor relieved to the General Inspector - 1923, 1925, 1927 and 1928
Register of Admissions of those entering the workhouse: 1923, 1924, 1926, 1927, 1928 and 1929
The Dudley Herald, 1926

From Devon Record Office, Exeter:
Workhouse Masters Report Book, 1920 - 29

Interview: Mrs Gladys Homer, 1987, Dudley

Secondary Sources:
The Workhouse system: M.A.Crofter Great Britain, 1981
The Land of Goshen — Totnes Workhouse, 1869: Totnes Community Archives, 1986: Anne German
The Dudley Union Workhouse 1856 - 1863: Margaret Gregory.
The Workhouse: Norman Longmate, 1974
The Battle against poverty, Vol 1: Brian Rodgers.
The good Town of Totnes: Russell and Phillips England, 1984
British Society 1914 - 45: John Stevenson, 1984
Devon: White, 1850.

Graph 1a: Weekly Returns of number of Poor Relieved to General Inspector, in and around area of Dudley Town, Dudley County, Sedgley, Cosley, Tipton, Rowly Regis.

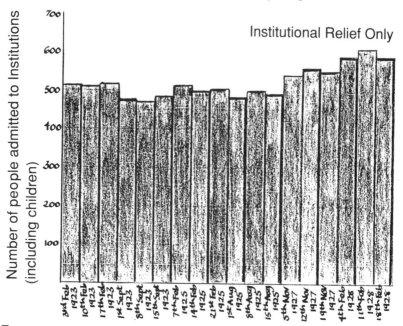

Graph 1b: Weekly returns of number of Poor Relieved to General inspector in and around area of Totnes

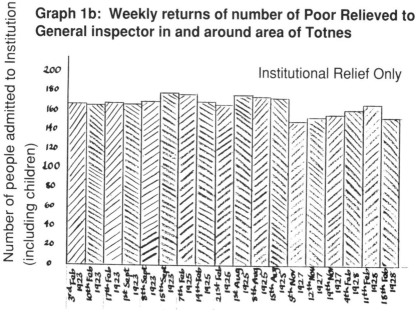

Graph 2a: **Weekly Returns of number of Poor Relieved to General Inspector in and around Dudley Town etc.**

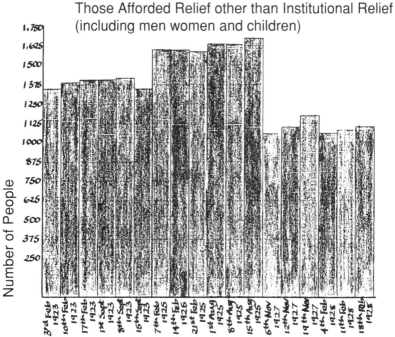

Those Afforded Relief other than Institutional Relief (including men women and children)

Graph 2b: Those Afforded Relief other than Institutional Relief (including men, women and children): Totnes

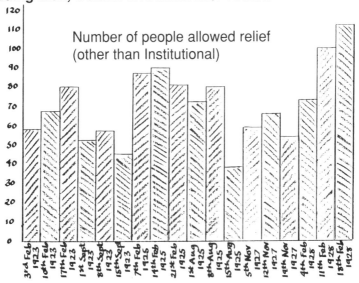

Number of people allowed relief (other than Institutional)

Graph 3a: Age Ratio of those who entered the workhouses in the Area of the Dudley Union
Covering the Periods of: Sept 1923; Feb 1924; Mar 1926; Sept 1927; Feb 1928

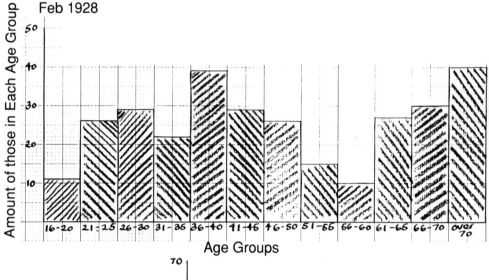

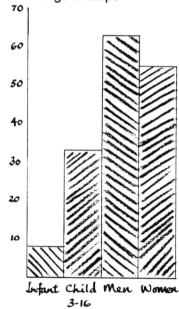

Graph 3b:
Average age groups of those entering the Workhouse
Covering the Periods of: Sept 1923; Feb 1924; Mar 1926; Sept 1927; Feb 1928

Graph 4a

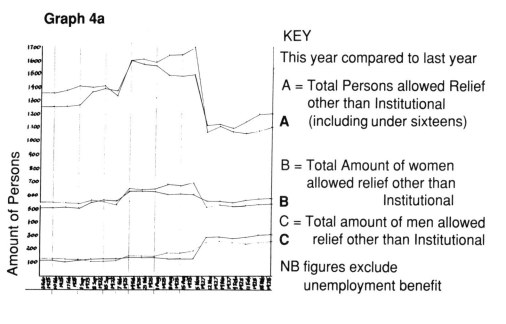

KEY

This year compared to last year

A = Total Persons allowed Relief
other than Institutional
A (including under sixteens)

B = Total Amount of women
allowed relief other than
B Institutional

C = Total amount of men allowed
C relief other than Institutional

NB figures exclude
unemployment benefit

Graph 4b: Totnes

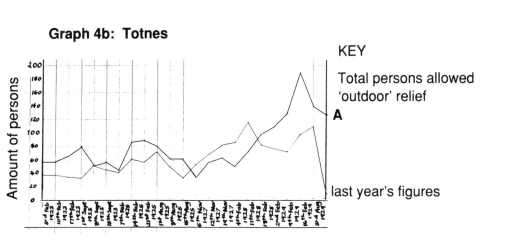

KEY

Total persons allowed
'outdoor' relief

A

last year's figures

Graph 5: Proportion of skilled workers compared to unskilled workers, entering the workhouses covering the period 1923-1929 (at various intervals) in the region of Dudley Union

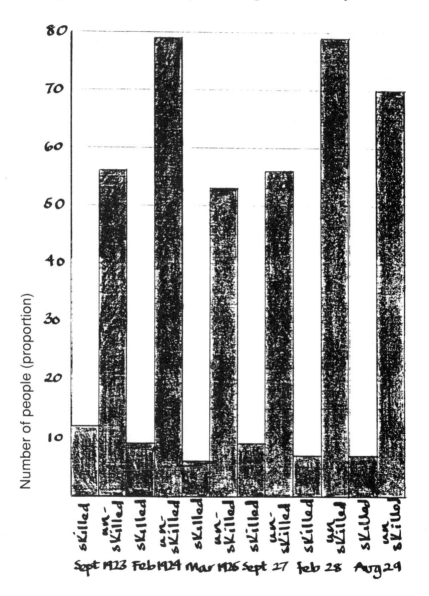